Dear Parent:
Your child's love of reading starts here!

Every child learns to read in a different way and at his or her own speed. Some go back and forth between reading levels and read favorite books again and again. Others read through each level in order. You can help your young reader improve and become more confident by encouraging his or her own interests and abilities. From books your child reads with you to the first books he or she reads alone, there are I Can Read Books for every stage of reading:

SHARED READING
Basic language, word repetition, and whimsical illustrations, ideal for sharing with your emergent reader

BEGINNING READING
Short sentences, familiar words, and simple concepts for children eager to read on their own

READING WITH HELP
Engaging stories, longer sentences, and language play for developing readers

READING ALONE
Complex plots, challenging vocabulary, and high-interest topics for the independent reader

ADVANCED READING
Short paragraphs, chapters, and exciting themes for the perfect bridge to chapter books

I Can Read Books have introduced children to the joy of reading since 1957. Featuring award-winning authors and illustrators and a fabulous cast of beloved characters, I Can Read Books set the standard for beginning readers.

A lifetime of discovery begins with the magical words "I Can Read!"

Visit www.icanread.com for information
on enriching your child's reading experience.

I Can Read Book® is a trademark of HarperCollins Publishers.

Mia and the Big Sister Ballet
Copyright © 2012 by HarperCollins Publishers
All Rights Reserved. Manufactured in China.
No part of this book may be used or reproduced in any manner whatsoever without written permission except in the case of brief
quotations embodied in critical articles and reviews. For information address HarperCollins Children's Books, a division of HarperCollins
Publishers, 195 Broadway, New York, NY 10007.
www.icanread.com
Library of Congress catalog card number: 2011927586
ISBN 978-0-06-173308-6 (trade bdg.) — ISBN 978-0-06-173307-9 (pbk.)
Book design by Sean Boggs
17 18   SCP   10 9 8 7 6 5 4 3 2
❖
First Edition

I Can Read!

SHARED My First READING

Mïa
and the
Big Sister Ballet

by Robin Farley
pictures by Aleksey and Olga Ivanov

HARPER
An Imprint of HarperCollinsPublishers

Mia is in the city!
Her dance class
is visiting the theater.

Mia's sister
will be there!

Mia's sister is named Ava.

Ava is a dancer!

Mia and her friends
watch Ava onstage.

Ava twirls and leaps.

She is a star!

The curtain closes.

Ava bows.

The class cheers!

Now Ava will show
the class a new dance!

Miss Bird takes the class
up to the stage.

Ava wears
blue toe shoes.
She has on a blue tutu.

"Let's dance!"

Ava says.

Mia watches Ava twirl.

Then Mia twirls.

Mia dances her best.

"Look, Ava!" she says.

But Ava is busy.

She is helping others.

Ava helps Anna point her toes.

Ava helps Ruby bend her legs
into a plié.

Ava helps Bella spring
into the air.

And Ava helps Tess spin
around and around.

But Ava doesn't help Mia.

And Ava doesn't see
Mia dance her best.

Mia is sad.
She sits down
on a bench.

She doesn't feel
like dancing anymore.

Ava sees Mia.
"Why don't you
want to dance?"
Ava asks.

"You were too busy
to watch me," Mia tells her.

"I was helping your friends,"
Ava tells Mia.
"I already know you're a star!"

Ava gives Mia a big hug!

"Will you dance with me?"

Ava asks.

The sisters dance together!

When she grows up
Mia is going to be
just like her big sister—
a dancing star!

Dictionary

Miss Bird's School of Dance

Theater

(you say it like this: the-a-ter)

A building where dancers perform

Plié

(you say it like this: plee-ay)

A dance position where you

bend at the knees

Toe Shoes

(you say it like this: tow shooz)

The shoes that ballet dancers wear